MODERN POETRY

ALSO BY DIANE SEUSS

frank: sonnets
Still Life with Two Dead Peacocks and a Girl
Four-Legged Girl
Wolf Lake, White Gown Blown Open
It Blows You Hollow

MODERN POETRY

poems

Diane Seuss

Graywolf Press

This publication is made possible, in part, by the voters of Minnesota through a Minnesota State Arts Board Operating Support grant, thanks to a legislative appropriation from the arts and cultural heritage fund. Significant support has also been provided by other generous contributions from foundations, corporations, and individuals. To these organizations and individuals we offer our heartfelt thanks.

Published by Graywolf Press
212 Third Avenue North, Suite 485
Minneapolis, Minnesota 55401

www.graywolfpress.org

Published in the United States of America
Printed in Canada

ISBN 978-1-64445-275-2 (cloth)
ISBN 978-1-64445-276-9 (ebook)

2 4 6 8 9 7 5 3 1
First Graywolf Printing, 2024

Library of Congress Control Number: 2023940112

Jacket design: Jeenee Lee

Jacket photo: Courtesy of the author

For my Reader

CONTENTS

❦

❦

❦

❦

❦

This morning Poetry has conquered—I have relapsed into those abstractions which are my only life—I feel escaped from a new strange and threatening sorrow—And I am thankful for it—

—*John Keats to John Hamilton Reynolds, 23 September 1818*

It must be this rhapsody or none,
The rhapsody of things as they are.

—*Wallace Stevens, "The Man with the Blue Guitar"*

My last defense
Is the present tense.

—*Gwendolyn Brooks, "Old Mary"*

MODERN POETRY

LITTLE FUGUE STATE

Far have I wandered not knowing
the names of where,
long have I woven this dress
of human hair, here
I have pitched my tent, here and there,
not knowing my name,
or where, not even the color of my hair
nor why
it tangles so, nor where my comb goes,
nor where my brush,
how far I wandered through underbrush,
into onrush,
nor where my body was, nor what it called
itself, nor the nature
of my calling, nor what my scrawling meant,
not that scrawl then,
nor this scrawl here, nor what a self
could be,
nor what a bee could be, nor breath,
nor poetry,
this dog I've walked and walked
to death.

CURL

No longer at home in the world
and I imagine
never again at home in the world.

Not in cemeteries or bogs
churning with bullfrogs.
Or outside the old pickle shop.
I once made myself
at home on that street,

and the street after that,
and the boulevard. The avenue.
I don't need to explain it to you.

It seems wrong
to curl now within the confines
of a poem. You can't hide
from what you made
inside what you made

or so I'm told.

BALLAD

Oh dream, why do you do me this way?
Again, with the digging, again with the digging up.
Once more with the shovels.
Once more, the shovels full of dirt.
The vault lid. The prying. The damp boards.

Mother beside me.
Like she's an old hat at this.
Like all she's got left is curiosity.
Like curiosity didn't kill the cat.
Such a sweet, gentle cat it was.

Here we go again, dream.
Mother, wearing her take-out-the-garbage coat.
I haven't seen that coat in years.
The coat she wore to pick me up from school early.
She appeared at the back of the classroom, early.

Go with your mother, teacher said.
Diane, you are excused.
I was a little girl. Already a famous actress.
I looked at the other kids. I acted lucky.
Though everyone knows what an early pickup means.

An early pickup, dream.
What's wrong, I asked my mother. It was early spring.
Bright sunlight. The usual birds.
Air, teetering between bearable and unbearable.
Cold, but not cold enough to shiver.

Still, dream, I shiver.
You know, my mother said.
Her long garbage coat flying.
There was a wind that day.
A wind like a scurrying grandmother, dusting.

Look inside yourself, my mother said.
You know why I have come for you.
And still I acted lucky. Lucky to be out.
Lucky to be out in the cold world with my mother.
I'm innocent, I wanted to say.

A little white girl, trying out her innocence.
A white lamb, born into a cold field.
Frozen almost solid. Brought into the house.
Warmed all night with hair dryers.
Death? I said. Smiling. Lucky.

We're barely to the parking lot.
Barely to the car ride home.
But the classroom already felt like the distant past.
Long ago, my classmates pitying me.
Arriving at this car full of uncles.

Were they wearing suits? Death such a formal occasion.
My sister, angry-crying next to me.
Me, encountering a fragment of evil in myself.
Evilly wanting my mother to say it.
What? I asked, smiling. My lamb on full display at the fair.

He's dead! my sister said. Hit me in the gut with her flute.
Her flute case. Her rental flute. He's dead!
Our father.
Our father, who we were not supposed to know had been dying.
He's dead! The flute gleaming in its red case.

Here, my mother said at home.
She'd poured us each a small glass of Pepsi.
We normally couldn't afford Pepsi.
Lucky, I acted.
He's no longer suffering, my mother said.

Here, she said. Drink this.
The little bubbles flew. They bit my tongue.
My evil persisted. What is death? I asked.
And now, dream, once more you bring me my answer.
Dig, my mother said. Pry, she said.

I don't want to see, dream.
The lid so damp it crumbled under my hands.
The casket just a drawerful of bones.
A drawerful. Just bones and teeth.
That one tooth he had. Crooked like mine.

LITTLE SONG

You can't stay vigilant and remain alive.
Or infinite vigilance is a kind of death.
Or you can't be present tense.
That is, tense about the present.
Here, you said in school. Present. But you were not.
Your mind back home eating sweet elephants from a jar.
Or placing Thumbelina in a milkweed car.

What luxury, to think of milkweed cars
and cookie jars and turning lights on in the dark
or lights off in the light or dreams of dropping
vigilance or memories of negligence, heedless
in your posh knee socks, your ritzy lamb, your
lush pop beads, your lilac jam, your breathless,
deathless, feckless little song.

MODERN POETRY

It was what I'd been waiting for my whole life,
but I wasn't ready for poetry. I didn't have
the tools. Roethke—
I appreciated the greenhouse poems,

and decades later saw his bed, toilet, upright
piano in that desolate town where he was raised,
not unlike the desolate town where I was raised.
No greenhouse in my town, but the Green Giant

factory, where mushrooms grew on cow shit.
Wallace Stevens—I wrote a paper on "Loneliness
in Jersey City" having no clue
what he meant by "The deer and the dachshund are one,"

and got an A anyway by faking it.
The professor made us read
"Sunday Morning," which struck me
as long. I couldn't focus yet, I was eighteen. A poem

against heaven, he told us. "Is there no change of death
in paradise? / Does ripe fruit never fall?" That I could
understand, having known some plums,
and that icky-sweet smell of a dead mouse in the wall.

Gerard Manley Hopkins—not modern per se,
but my professor said, one of the first modernists,
so what did modern poetry really mean? Maybe
just fucked up, as Hopkins was for sure, and tongue

twistery, and depressed, Jesuit, maybe bipolar.
I stared at his photograph, the long nose and cleft
in his chin, noticed that even in "No worst, there is none"
he had the wherewithal to put in the accent marks

to school us as to how to hear the thing. And WCW,
Williams, my roommate and I called him Billy C. Billygoat—
I knew something of wheelbarrows, old women,
and as I said, plums, but the prof showed us

how complicated it all really was, the whole "no ideas
but in things" thing, the near rhymes,
depends and *chickens* and *red*, again, I was not yet
capable of being smart and wondered if I ever would be,

though I kept getting A's on the papers, maybe
because the professor felt sorry for me, and I'm not
just saying that. The final modern poet was Sylvia Plath—
a woman, blonde, and I didn't trust blondes,

smart, angry, angry at men, I was told, depressed, cheated
on, dead. I imagined her being in Modern Poetry with us,
mopping the floor with us, with her developed
mind, her ooh and ahh sounds, her thesis, "The Magic Mirror,"

on the double in Dostoevsky. I pictured her calling me
a charlatan, like Gaylord did in class the week we studied her.
He called her a charlatan psychopath, and me a charlatan
for sticking up for her. I had to go back

to the dorm and look up *charlatan* in the dictionary.
A fraud, the dictionary said. A quack, which yes, I was,
though so was Gaylord. Who isn't a quack at eighteen?
I wanted to love Sylvia, but to love her would mean

loving someone who would have hated me.
It would be a few years, after I flunked out
of college, until I took a class called Women's Literature
at the public university down the hill with a teacher

named Stephanie, who looked a lot like Françoise Sagan,
teenage author of *Bonjour Tristesse*, but older and with a cap
of gray hair. Margaret Atwood. Toni Morrison. Adrienne Rich.
Charlotte Perkins Gilman. Plath. Sexton. Lorde.

Kate Chopin. Alice Walker. Djuna Barnes. I was beginning
to understand, but barely. To ask a pertinent question
now and then, like where the hell was Langston Hughes
in Modern Poetry? Dickinson, in Nineteenth Century American Lit?

If Hopkins was a modernist, how about Dickinson,
with her weird rhymes and what Galway Kinnell called
her "inner, speech-like, sliding, syncopated rhythm,"
a counterpoint to her iambic lines? A horse straining at the bit

in the direction of free verse. A woman who drove
a motorcycle to Women's Literature, wore a fringed
black leather jacket, and worked at the Kalamazoo airport
in the booth where people pay for parking was shot and killed there

by her ex-boyfriend. From then on, the class became
something else. Stephanie had us over to her house,
a damp place in the woods. She roasted a goat
and served it to us, shredded, on blue plates.

The books had become more, and less, important.
We spoke of them, huddled on the floor by the fire.
I remember most of all the bushel baskets
of apples and grapes for winemaking, drawing fruit flies.

I'm not complaining. It was all more than I deserved.
The goat. The greenhouse. The liberated blonde badass
on her motorcycle. *Sula. Surfacing.* "Sunday Morning."
Ripe plums. My education.

COLETTE

I went through a Colette stage, did you?
Chéri, The Last of Chéri.
When I say *Gigi* I don't mean the supermodel.
I mean a novella by Colette.
Waist-length hair. Pert mouth.
Locked in a room by her first husband
until she produced enough pages to be liberated
for the evening. And then—get ready to be irked—
he published her novels under his own name.

You know the type? You know the type.
You know it's snowing? It's snowing.
To explain Colette is like rowing a heavy boat
across a cold lake whose far shore I can't even
begin to conceptualize.
It was a form of liberation,
writing of courtesans and gigolos.
Cutting off one's fat rope of hair. So fat,
it was said, so heavy, the braid required its own chair.

Colette sporting a men's suit. Musty. Frowsy.
I lived alone when I read Colette.
Picked small apples off a tree and ate them
in two chomps, like a horse.
The house had no running water. No power.
It was kerosene or sit in the dark.
Wood or freeze. Outhouse with squirrels
and wolf spiders. Colette with her gray scrawl
of hair. Her hands twisted with arthritis.

Vanity bruised. Hers or mine? We're made
of the same meat. Little bow of a mouth
intact, but pulled a bit too tight with bitterness.
Her cigarette smoke so omnipresent
it was like a bent wire over her head.

To give you Colette I must limp across the century
wearing flimsy lace slippers. Just read her.
Just stare at the photographs. Then consult
Barthes's *Camera Lucida*. You will need him

in order to see what seeing her really means.
Then live without deodorant. Then pee in a hole
in the ground. Stack your books on a small raw wooden table
you found in a sweet-potato field crawling with snakes.
Chéri, The Last of Chéri, Gigi, piled on a confiscated table.
Colette was an abhorrent kitten with a bony nose
and a thick jaw who died on a fur couch, talking
to herself. Even her book covers were ugly,
at least the editions I managed to buy used,

or steal. What kind of person steals books?
The kind who robs the apple tree of its apples.

MY EDUCATION

Not just what I feel but what I know
and how I know it, my unscholarliness,
my rawness, all rise out of the cobbled
landscape I was born to. Those of you
raised similarly, I want to say: this is not
a detriment and it is not a benefit. It only is,
it is, like a cobbled house is, fieldstones
and mortar, slipshod, spare parts welded
crookedly, crudely but cleverly, skinny
iron winding staircase leading to the attic
bolted on both ends, and up there, a gap
in the window where the snow comes in
and architects a little drift on the bed.
And meals were cobbled. Kernels on the cob
haphazardly arranged, not lined up in military
rows, and sometimes a row was not filled in
at all, and your teeth, when biting down,
met an emptiness. And shotgun pellets
in the rabbit meat. Stray hobnail dishes, studded,
rescued from an abandoned house on fire,
in an array of jewel tones, would appear
without warning on the table. A blood-colored
butter dish, yellow perch on a cobalt-blue platter
encircled in fried egg sacs. Or ducks or a pheasant
thrown erratic on the back porch, payment
for something given or not taken.
When I'd been away and returned, I could see,
freshly, the cobbled lushness of the trees,
and the arbitrary drift of brown spots
on the white cows in the meadows,
and the wireworm-filled tunnels in the morels
at the base of dead cherry trees. The cemetery
is unsystematic, as is the library, graves scattered
like chicken feed, books strewn on old tables
from canceled Sunday school classrooms. I loved

books but learned very little in school. I could read,
so the reading instruction drove me nearly mad,
and I plugged my ears, first with my hands
until I was caught, then with something I could do
inside my head that muffled the teacher's voice
like she was speaking into a canning jar.
What I know of literature, of history, is spotty.
I was a poor student, disengaged from the things
I didn't need, and I knew what I needed,
and that the time to get it was now.
When I needed Keats, I got him. I read enough
to get the point, then tuned in to his ghost.
I read most of Joseph Conrad, having figured out
that I could find some things repulsive and still
require them for my project. My project
was my life. There was no vision or overarching
plan. There was only foraging for supplies,
many of which were full of worms or covered
in dust, like apples on the orchard floor,
and furniture junked on the side of the road.
Have you ever seen a pie cooling on the sill
and found yourself hungry enough to steal it?
Or does that only happen in picture books?
If you are like me, to learn of the gods you must
beg, borrow, or steal. Eavesdrop, as gossip
is sagacity, a word I learned from Emily
Dickinson. Don't underestimate direct
experience. Ants know earth. Dragonflies
know air. A cobbled mind is not fatal.
You have to be willing to self-educate
at a moment's notice, and to be caught
in your ignorance by people who will
use it against you. You will mispronounce
words in front of a crowd. It cannot be
avoided. But your poems, with all of their
deficiencies, products of lifelong observation
and asymmetric knowledge, will be your own.

Built on the edge of tradition, they will
rarely be anthologized. I have camped
at this outpost my whole life, as did my mother,
who slept on sugar sacks in the basement
or on the front porch, in early spring,
when snow still clumped around fugitive
crocuses, just to keep herself forsaken.

JUKE

What kind of juke do you prefer?
For me, it's the kind with three
songs and thirty-seven blank
title strips. Three songs, and two
are "Luckenbach, Texas."
The third is beautiful and arcane,
but the patrons hate it,
and the record skips.
I prefer the three-song juke
and the three-toothed human

smile. I found the juke of my dreams
in a bar called "Chums," no clue
the origin or meaning
of the quotation marks. It was a prime
number of a bar, and now it's dead.
One night, drinking half-and-
halfs, half beer, half tomato juice,
with schnapps chasers, a cheap
source of hallucination.
A soon-to-be-defrocked Catholic

priest, Vic Jr., my mother, and me,
our faces streaked blue with pool
chalk, juke red as a beating heart,
and just a strip of hollyhocks
and a tree line between us
and the northern lights.
I was young. I looked like a Rubens
painting of a woman half-eaten
by moths. What lucky
debauchery, the ride back

on a washboard dirt road,
taking everything for granted,
flipping off the aurora borealis
like it was some three-toothed human
in flashy clothes dancing
to get my attention.
I wasn't a mean drunk then,
just honest.
Next morning, mom walked in
on the naked priest

in the shack's garage,
washing himself with a rag
and cold water from the well
in a metal dishpan. I'd later do dishes
in that pan and wash my hair
in that pan. We popped popcorn
on the one-burner wood-burning
stove and ate it out of that pan.
I'm talking about a time and a place.
All I can say of it is that it was real.

The song choices were limited,
so the grooves were dug deep.

POP SONG

I met my father again in a video store by the creamery,
in a record store on my lunch break, in a museum whisper booth,
in Washington Square performing with a Beatles cover band,
and he said to me, Di, he said, you're not what I expected,

like an online date who doesn't think you measure up
to the photograph. I think he meant I turned out differently
than he imagined when I was three and I'd already learned
to read the newspaper. Di, he said, and I saw in his face,

well, what father would want me for a daughter?
It was as if God looked upon creation and wondered
at its atrocities. How, God thinks, could I
have fucked up so badly, but keeps it to himself.

Di, my father said, we were in the lamb barn of a county fair.
The lambs' fleece was matted. They bleated piteously.
My father hadn't aged a day, black hair combed into a wave
in the front you could lose yourself in. Children are known

to accept their parents' hairstyles without question, no basis,
yet, to judge. I'm not sure he was glad to see me. To a dead man,
a living adult daughter must be such an overwhelm, a real load,
and from death he had learned to prefer simplicity, the ephemera

of steam rising from a cup, birds, but he didn't care what kind
of birds. He was wearing a humble but clean shirt. He wanted,
I believe, to keep it that way. I was like a cake
with too many ingredients that had overflowed its pan, spilled

into the oven, and smoldered there. Di, he said.
I could tell he had a mint lozenge in his mouth.
One of those that winnows but never really goes away.
It wasn't a lamb barn after all,

where we met up, it was a diner, and he did a spin
on his stool at the counter as if to entertain me, as fathers
are apt to do, or so I've been told. It's too late for me
to be beautiful, I said, the ruin too vast,

for I assumed he wanted beauty. Don't fathers want beauty
from their daughters? How ashamed
he was at my exploits. A nuanced man had lost, in death,
all nuance. In fact, the dead don't love the living.

Like Jesus, they judge us.
Di, was all he said. Nice to see you.

BALLAD FROM THE SOUNDHOLE OF AN UNSTRUNG GUITAR

The best I ever wrote was in an attic.
No chair. Manual typewriter on an upended box.
No screen on the lone window, which I removed.
Bats flew through.

I woke up one night and Blue was in bed with me.
Nah, I said, and he put on his wire-rimmed glasses and left.
Somehow, I ended up with two kittens. Littermates.
I wonder how they lived and died, where they went.

The only furniture was the mattress on the floor.
A wooden box full of someone's Mardi Gras beads.
No ethics. No lock on the door.
No worries about vermin, rabies, fleas.

Where did I pee in the middle of the night?
There must have been a bathroom down those narrow stairs.
A shower somewhere.
A gold shower curtain laced with mold.

Blue once told me I walked in on him peeing and I laughed.
That it ruined his life.
Well, Jesus, I'm sorry.
I would never have apologized back then.

I knew no forms.
Just a swarm of bees in the rafters who agreed to leave me be.
I made a line break when I took a drag on my Salem Light.
Menthols were pure as poetry.

Where are the words now, that you wrote in that hellhole?
On the typewriter ribbon I stuck in a knothole.

COMMA

To never be touched again. That line
has a sound. Hear it?
I don't want to bring a story
to it. Not even an image.
It has a sound. Listen.

To never be touched. Oh, a nurse,
a doctor, but never to be touched in that way.
You know what way. Listen.
Hear it. Let's not tag it with a feeling.
Give me a break. What possible song

would you play when you toss my ashes,
someone once asked me.
There is no song, he said. Don't
narrativize, Diane. Don't narrativize Diane.
See what a comma can do?

MONODY

Kindness, like enthralling
madness
after shock
treatments, is first to go.
In the past, I snapped
the beans' spines, aware
that something died
so I could thrive.
But this emptiness
makes even a nightingale
consumable. As for
the song and red tailfeathers,
take them, here.
I just don't care.
To grieve is a dilettantish
stand-in for the subject
of my grief. What I'm saying
is the verb
is a canned performance
of the missing noun.
Or I'm saying
I don't know how
to feel anymore.
Use metaphor,
but don't adhere to her.
As more than once
I was used but not adored.

VILLANELLE

I dreamed I was reading a villanelle
in front of a crowd. Next to me on the floor
was a large bag of garbage I'd mistakenly
brought with me onto the stage. My own garbage.

And the crowd did not care about the villanelle.
Its intricacies or its subject, which was ornate
and thorny and probably none of my business.
I was a snob in the midst of a throng of people

hungry only for the truth. I have never played
the role of a snob or read a bad poem
into a microphone next to a sack of my own
garbage, in life or dream. What do you think

it means? Are the gods mocking me for acting
in-the-know? This would happen back home a lot.
Anybody who tooted their own horn
or dared to sound as if they were an expert

on any subject were mocked and driven
into the next county. Never hold yourself above.
There is no expertise. There is only good sense,
earned hard and held close to the vest.

It is not to be displayed but hoarded,
like canned goods in a storm cellar.
Go back for the garbage and deal with it.
In so doing, if you rouse a swarm of flies,

they're yours to tolerate or swat. Choose
your poison, but don't poison the well.
Your dreams are just dreams,
and all dreams go up in smoke.

FOLK SONG

Let me enter the afterlife lithe not plodding.
Rise out of this heavy peasantry. Lithe
and cool as a battery-powered flame,
not fire. My feet
are short and wide. The soles, stained
with mulberries. I have never been lithe,
streamlined, pedicured, compressed, minimal, ergonomic,

silver
fuselage cutting the air.
In my herringbone skirt and shirttail out, I am a slob.
What is a slob but a knob of thickness, a mushroom
stem, a beer stein Mozart stole from the Hofbräuhaus while writing
Idomeneo.
My stylist, gravity. Memory a tree so loaded with fruit and birds the tips

of the branches rake the ground.
By lithe I do not mean in body, do I?
Do I mean in soul?
To be one of those green-eyed ones others refer to as
aquamarine. Empty
of ancestors. Face clean
of lipstick smears and other gestures of artifice.

Feet a rare triple-A, so narrow there aren't shoes
that won't chafe. Skin easy to tear,
like Kleenex we turned into carnations for parade floats.
Those drinks from the soda fountain we called Green Rivers.
Green and sweet, without flavor, but delicious.
I am too tired to hold up this heavy self.
Of selfhood I worked so hard to earn. Of work I worked so hard

to avoid. Of the working class. My class. Its itches and psychological riches.
Its notions and values and humble achievements.
Of this town which inhabitants speak of with endearments

as if it were a child. As if it's not like every other brat.
Town with its river, drunk on itself. Its shitty Xmas ornaments
and fall-down-fucked-up Santa on a raft tethered to the river bank.
Its tiny museum

built around the star of the show, a lamb born with two heads.
Every town has a two-headed something. It doesn't mean
anything.
You know what? I want to be rich and lithe.
Rich, with a lyric gift and a song
like a white-throated sparrow. I am vulture-heavy.
My stories are caskets filled with black feathers,

the lids pounded shut with railroad spikes.
The gravedigger is noodling Melba, the widow-woman,
and a hognose is consuming a toy train on cemetery lane.
Let me resurrect beyond the bracken
fronds and the three-legged stool and catgut guitar
and this two-ton song from the mouth
of a wax museum troubadour.

BLUISH

I bought a blue
knife. I couldn't help
myself. It did not change
my life. It cut
the same as any other
knife, though blue,
which for a while felt new,
and I could define myself,
if I needed to,
as a person who
chose a blue knife, who
lived with a blue knife, who
cut quite a figure
with her blue
knife, though it was ordinary
in every way beyond its hue.
I have a drawerful
of knives like other knives,
and some of them cut surprisingly
well, straight through.
But know me not by my blood
but by my blue. Have you
seen, my true ally, the inside of an ambulance?
It is not dim as you
might think. Not pink. Not thin. It is bright
white as wedding cake, as school glue.
Everything shows. Your newish tattoo.
Your lips, that gruesome pool-cue-
chalk blue.
The spinning light on top
of the ambulance is blue,
the color of a bruise.
Inside, Diane, you suffer,
and your suffering is you.

BALLAD IN SESTETS

I would like to have better ideas
than the ideas I have.
There is an idea I'm reaching for
but like a jar on the top shelf
and no step stool, I can't leap
to it.

Whatever it is, I can't leap to it.
I have been in large spaces.
Spaces too cavernous for ideas.
Too enormous, with rock faces,
cliffs and towers of sheer red
rock,

or enormous Virgin Marys, flying
buttresses, naves, transepts, rose
windows, chancels, stratospheric
crucifixes, where ideas
are snuffed out like altar
candles.

Snuffed and alone in cavernous spaces.
Alone, a misnomer. A word whose
definition I had to find in a dictionary.
Language comes hard. Silence corsets
me. In other words, I can't reach it,
the jar

on the shelf, or climb the sheer face
of the rock stained red by sunset,
or corner and pocket the miniscule
priest. It's beyond what I'm made of.
It matters how and where you are made,
and what

materials were at hand for the makers.
To say that I am alone is a misnomer.
Whatever I am, alone
doesn't cover it. What I am, I
am subsumed by it. It is
pleasant

to be without edges. To be a cloud
in a voluminous sky. I have been
in minimal spaces. Closer to anthill
than cavern or villa. Or tucked inside
the incalculable. A bead swallowed
by a whale,

sloughed-off sequin in a warehouse.
A jelly jar, a jar filled with pigs' feet,
lost in the giant's pantry.
Once there was a honeymoon.
The bride swang, or swung, out over
deep water.

No bells rang or rung.
It was a honeymoon, a minor chord
tucked inside a philharmonic.
It was cold and dark and wind and stars.
The closest neighbors were far.
They shone,

they shined their headlights
in the window of the shack, the hovel,
the villa, and delivered unto the couple
a loaf of bread still warm
from the kiln, from a witch's oven,
and soft

and golden-crusted and steam
rising from it like a blowhole blowing
spray or a chimney or pipe
blowing smoke, or a newborn birthed
in an icy field, steam spiraling
from the gash

of its open mouth like it had just taken
a drag from its first cigarette
and exhaled the smoke into the jar
of air, it's inexplicable,
there is no theory or idea or blanket
to cover it.

THRENODY

I don't cry on the outside.
I haven't reached that level of liberation
from the granite my angel is trapped in.
I do cry inside. Imagine taking a sunset cruise
and watching purple waves brew.
That's what I do.

Tears make the boat lurch.
Violet waves, they claw the shore.
Silly, to write of tears.
Small as drops of oil in a cold pan.
As grains of rice, or lice,
or misplaced punctuation

in a poorly worded entreaty pleading
for mercy. Ministers
used to say that without release (I'm trying
to be clean here) men would explode
and die. According to witches, the same
can be said of tears. An insipid subject

for poetry. I wrote a poem about that word,
insipid, so long ago it could have been penned
by a cherub etched on the sarcophagus
of a child. But the dead, in their vast
merriment, egg me on. Write the motherfucking
poem. See why I love them?

And why my big body holds not a pond
or an inland lake but an unabridged salt green sea?
Swells taller than Gothic cathedrals.
Pretty people dressed in chartreuse evening wear
dancing like eels through the matroneum.
The music of sea-roar,

and the Reagan-era deinstitutionalized,
wearing seaweed hospital gowns, set loose
in a concert hall blowing into their enormous
wind instruments. Do you carry
this grief inside yourself too? No,
I imagine you say. But you do.

CODA

The best poem is no poem.
In a swath of poems, or a swathe of poems,
the best poem is without genealogy or fragrance.

It's like an animal born without a voice box.
Or its inconvenient voice box has been removed.

The best body, nobody says to no one, is no body.
The best body, no body at all.
The sound a bodiless body makes

is akin to the sound a bird makes when it dips
its beak into a cup of jam.

Sometimes a bone makes a sound when it breaks.
It sounds just as you'd imagine it would sound.
Other times the bone is as quiet

as a really good burglar breaking and entering.
There used to be a prairie that extended way past

the ending of every story. An expanse of sedges and grasses
and wind, which made a sound like a sprinkler when the water
has been turned off for the nonpayment of the bill.

The what? The bill. The unpaid water bill. Out of the spigot
streams a thirsty noncompliance. An antisong.

AN ARIA

How do I get my mind back? Yes, my mind.
The fascist, that murderer of half a million,
never had my body.
My body has been owned, but not by him.

I never liked backtracking.
Brush Road, Born Street.
I've walked those roads before, barefoot.
There is no going back to Born.

No mind left behind to recoup.
It's like donated clothes you try to buy back
from the sucker who's already wearing them.
But there is something to be claimed.

Some comrade to bust out of jail
who can't see the way forward
even when you crack the chains.
In my pre-tit days, I'd walk to the empty outdoor

theater and sit on the playground equipment
beneath the screen. Everything in that place
was silver. Gravel, playground horses, and rocket ships
whose paint had chipped away by wind and time.

I knew nothing larger than that screen.
No god so sublime. Silver-white against the whiter clouds.
Peppered with purple bird shit.
When night falls, anything can project itself

against a face like that. Cartoons, or *Vixen*, rated X.
When the free-show man
came to town, he'd hang
a sheet between two trees

and project cowboy movies against it.
Kids sat on the grass eating popcorn
from greasy paper bags, watching ads
scroll down the screen.

Popcorn wasn't free.
A free show is never really free.
Do you think someone didn't die
on that sheet hung between two trees?

I once received a letter
from the current lover of the love
of my life telling me he'd overdosed and died.
She wrote on thin blue paper etched with flowers.

An act of grace I hadn't earned.
I'd left him behind
knowing it was just a matter of time.
My mind has grown wooden around love,

like a tree that has nearly swallowed
a garden
gate where lovers met at moonrise
when the air was thick with Hesperis.

A musty, fatal scent, like punks
who refused to bathe.
Lovers long dead, gate
now opening only to the tree's heartwood.

My son's first love was Anne Frank,
after he read her diary. He was eight,
drawing portraits of her day and night.
I must have Anne, he said when I tucked him in,

though he knew she was dead, whatever that means.
This is the mind, sepia, color of dried blood.
Maybe the first love is the best love.
The first loss, the worst. If so, mine came early.

The rest is repetition compulsion,
iterations until the ink runs dry.
Still, remembering wakes my mind a little,
or some facsimile of the mind I used to be.

All activities of the mind now seem quaint,
like dolls with lace faces unearthed
from beneath the attic stairway.
My feelings, too, smothered like a kingdom

of bees so the buzzing
doesn't draw attention to their honey.
Now, to unmuffle myself, I read Keats's love letters,
written in a tubercular fever, then listen

to *Marquee Moon*, album by Television,
that Tom Verlaine band,
so aggressive live it made me start my period,
leave a lyric bloodstain on the chair.

Then I play "Gimme Shelter" on repeat to be awash
in the supremacy of Merry Clayton's background vocals.
Called into the studio in the middle of the night, cold,
hair in curlers, pregnant, pushed out her scream-

song aria three times, and miscarried a daughter
the next day. She blamed it on the song
but not her voice. When she woke after a car accident,
years later, with amputated legs, she asked only

about her voice. Mother, may I sing again?
May I see again, not a symbol of a flower but Hesperis,
tolls again in the wind again. Flower of an hour.
A fragrant hour. Its face, skin, smile,

its opening again, the curtain of petals
closing over its face again.
May I take the murdered world in?
Sing of it again?

ALLEGORY

I loved the north. I remember that.
The quality of light, yet I don't have the will
to describe it. Thimbleberries,
like things out of fairy tales.
Green water overpowering the night.
That impersonal bashing sound.
Cold fingers combing through stones.
Looking for something. I don't remember
what. Blue fingers. Lips.
A blue garment I called my power shirt.
Green-blue. Big enough it floated in the wind
and barely touched me. Grief
that I had to leave and everything
leaving represented, an ache
in my guts, work, a premonition, but still
the belief I would one day return.
It would all be here waiting for me,
unchanged. But even the body
of water grows tired of itself.

⤳

I yearned only for what I had.
I am tempted to list those things,
but the time for listing is over.
I'll mention that there was a monastery.
Monks with long beards who made jam
from wild berries and baked heavy
loaves of bread. In their literature
they wrote of winter as their season of suffering.
There are worse things than winter, I wanted to say,
handing them money for bread.
I wanted to lift my shirt and show them my long scar.
When I was still bleeding, I changed my tampon
in the woods behind the monastery and left

the used one behind like the scat of a wild animal.
Blood in the air, the scent of it like wet pennies.
Tearing into those loaves.
The wind with its one-track mind.
It had broken me down and starved me.

～

It was a place filled with plotless stories,
music without melody.
How can I explain. I'm sure you've heard
discordant music, but that's not what I mean.
And you've read stories in which nothing happens.
Maybe composed of a series of low-grade epiphanies.
Or flamboyant description that in the end comes to nothing.
Sooner or later, those authors all died of syphilis.
The tubercular ones were the meaning-makers,
as if meaning would keep them alive.
But meaning, in a gale, is the first to go.
In the north, all forms stood for themselves.
There was no need to fill them with anything.
Chalices in which wine would be superfluous.
And every moment a form, a string of tongueless bells.

～

There is a poetry of rage and a poetry of hope.
Each fuels the other, looks in the mirror and sees
the other. Or wields the other. Isn't it funny
to imagine hope, not much more than a toddler,
wielding rage in its fist like a cudgel?
When I was in college and working on a paper
about Hawthorne's story "My Kinsman, Major
Molineux," I had to find *cudgel* in a dictionary.
We were to explicate the symbol of the cudgel.
Later it would be the gold doubloon in *Moby-Dick*.
What is *explicate*, I wondered. What is *cudgel*?

Dictionaries then were musty and heavy and old.
You had to go to them. They did not come to you.
When I was north, I read books with flimsy pages.
Books without symbols. Only facts.
And photographs, not drawings.
I did not have to rise to them, or kneel at their feet.
When the house burned, struck
by lightning, they burned with it.

     ∽

The air in the north was cold and thin.
There were enemies but not tyrants then.
Ghost towns and towns. Ships and shipwrecks.
Ships and mirages of ships.
Who could tell the difference?
A herd of white deer whose ghosts,
after the deer were shot, looked as they had in life,
white, their eyes rimmed pink.
Sandhill cranes flew over,
their calls like bones rattling in a wooden box.
It seemed as if one gravedigger covered the whole region,
his face bashed in by his own shovel.
At a bar called "Chums" I shot
pool with the locals, drank myself under the table.
Whatever filled my glass was colorless and lethal.
No one spoke to me, as people in the north
did not speak to strangers, and I was a stranger.
One murky country song played over and over
until I began to believe it was the only song in the world.
During the day, the light in the trees was green-gold.
That's all I'm going to say about it.
There are too many poems about light.

     ∽

Whatever the north was, I miss it.
My life since has grown thick without it.
Thick, like sorghum syrup, with experience.
Heavy with memory's tonnage, such a drag, such a load.
It has no place here. Be, or leave.
I wish I was less, a recipe composed of a single ingredient.
I once knew a singer with a voice like that.
The high, thin sound of the white plastic flutes
we were forced to play in elementary school.
Each note the same as the last,
and each instrument the same as the next,
like a lineup of factory-raised chicken eggs.
The thin-voiced singer moved to Ireland.
Bartended. Smoked a pack a day.
Some would say her voice was ruined,
husky now, dragging itself through the lower registers.
Many thought we looked alike, but I couldn't see it.
Now that her long hair is frizzed by time,
her garden unruly, her hem scraping the floor,
and her voice raw and low as something that echoes up
from an open pit mine, I see the resemblance.

In the north, there was not much to buy and little to sell
but for bread, and jam, and meat pies wrapped in wax paper.
I collected materials from the woods floor
and using a toy hammer and tiny gold nails
built a boat that would carry a message out into water.
I enjoyed building it and composing the message,
which was not unlike every other message sent into water.
It was a child's message, really.
I rolled it into a scroll, and encased it in a plastic film canister,
and attached it to the boat with waterproof wood glue,
but as soon as I launched it into deep water,
and watched it drift and bob toward sunset,
I lost faith in it, or interest.

Once it sailed away, it seemed to have little to do with me,
or nothing at all to do with me.

෴

During the plague,
which has become a way of life,
I collected the ends of bars of Ivory soap,
worn too thin for bathing or handwashing,
but useful maybe later when things like soap
begin to disappear off grocery shelves,
or what's left of the money dries up.
I imagined tethering the scraps together
with rubber bands I've saved and lassoed
to the glass door handle that leads to the attic.
One long winter of the plague, a raccoon lived
there, in the attic. I could hear its claws as it wandered
in circles over my head. My ceiling, its floor.
I know you've lived it, too. You understand
that you can cross a hundred bridges,
but there is no way to go north again,
by which I mean it's time to put to bed,
like the row of the giant's children
in their matching nightcaps,
our allegories of innocence.

WEEDS

The danger
of memory is going
to it for respite. Respite risks
entrapment, which is never
good. Don't debauch
yourself by living
in some former version of yourself
that was more or less naked.
Maybe it felt better then, but you were
not better. You were smaller, as the rain
gauge must fill to the brim
with its full portion of suffering.

What can memory be in these terrible times?
Only instruction. Not a dwelling.

Or if you must dwell:
The sweet smell of warm weeds then.
The sweet smell of warm weeds now.
An endurance. A standoff. A rest.

ANOTHER BALLAD

You're not old, I say to the old dog.
You're handsome, and you will never die.
He growls at me to establish his waning dominance.

You are the king, I say. A ruthless king.
Why do I speak to the dog, you ask.
Why do I write of the dog.

Because long ago I took myself out of the running
for human company,
like my mother before me, who never again

wore a dress or skirt after my father escaped
this mortal coil. Never another
dress or skirt. Like my mother before me,

I took myself out of the running,
no longer dressing to seduce via my own brand
of seduction. I was never seductive

in the traditional sense, but in the untraditional sense,
I knew how to wield seduction.
It had its day, let me say.

Let me say I wielded it effectively enough
to draw in a baseball player, a football player
twenty years my junior, a used-car salesman,

a pimp, a smelly old boss, a cardiologist,
and an old minister, who broke
into my house under the guise of needing a cup

of cool water, all to tell me what I do to men.
You know, he said, what you do to men.
You know what you do to men.

It worked until it didn't. It worked when I was,
for a time, the princess of a hive
of pansexual filmmakers. I hate her,

a woman director said when I appeared
on screen, I hate her. But she didn't hate me.
My blue cotton pants bought on the street

in Afghanistan had done their trick.
My pants, bought from a man without arms
or legs who rolled over the streets on a skateboard.

Indigo pants, with a drawstring.
They did their work for a hot minute.
They did not work on Tom, who only

liked women who looked like him.
Who can blame him? I don't blame him.
Had I been Tom, I would seek only myself

in the mirrors of other faces. He's dead now.
He died, no matter how many women
in whose faces he found himself.

Is he seducible now?
Are the dead seducible? The answer is no.
Once they escape this mortal coil? No.

The dead are inured to seduction. Believe me,
I've tried. I've worn the pants
sold by the armless man. He took

the cash with his teeth. He, too, was inured
to contrivances. Charms I have since
given up willingly. Age did not steal them.

I could still give it a go. No, I gave up every charm
on that bracelet willingly. Snipped them away
with wire cutters. Donated each to a different lake

or river which swallowed them like a fish
swallows the hook. Yes, I hooked, in my time,
a river. A lake. I hooked a whole town,

my hometown, to which I returned
like a conquering hero on July 4, 1976,
for the bicentennial celebration.

I wore what I wore. Shimmered and bangled.
Somehow, against the whole town, I won
the tug-of-war. I had no upper-body strength,

no lower-body strength, but by sheer power
of personality, defiance, shimmer,
I won the bicentennial tug-of-war. Still, all of that

I rescinded. Rescinded it like a bad law.
Wire-cut the charms. Each and every one.
Seeded every lake and river with the old tools

of my trade, as lakes and rivers are stocked
with fish so that they will grow up to be hooked.
Sad, isn't it? Both the fish's story and my own.

Both are stories of subterfuge, illusion.
Empty, but in a good way? Not in a good way.
Empty, like an undistinguished bottle.

Like one of my grandfather's whiskey bottles,
drained of its minimal magic. Maybe he escaped
his misery for a hot second. What misery?

Oh, the usual. A Jehovah's Witness wife
who converted late in the game. Loved
her son more than her husband.

Couldn't cook, all the poultry
raw at the joints. Made one good dish.
Sauerbraten. Then the son died and she tried

to climb in the casket. All to say, no wonder
he drained the bottle. No wonder the bottle
was empty. No wonder my mother donated

her orange skirt to Goodwill. Her black
skirt. My sister donated her pink bikini.
The one she bled through.

No wonder I talk
to the dog the way I do.
Lie as I do to the dog.

You will never die, I say.
You are young. Your coat is not gray.
You do not limp. You smell like fresh hay.

LITTLE REFRAIN

More and more I am surrounded
by it. The mind
and face of it.
The school and cult of it.
I once found it mysterious.
What's in the casket, you know.
What's in grandma's
basket.

In my skull I'd narrate
their heartache trapped inside
the box. Open your
mouth, here's some cream,
you know? And when I slept,
they populated, like wasps do
underpants on the line,
my dreams.

Its exoticized velvets aren't exotic.
Its silks aren't silk. The skull stains
the rayon pillow. That's as far
as it goes. Someone
is not knocking to get out.
Only melting into the woodwork,
you know.

At this late date I yearn
for its opposite. Honey-streaming
combs. Greenery. Some sort
of flowering vine climbing a small
dead chair. My god,
I'm homesick for life, the warm
snout of it, you know?

COWPUNK

Do you think your suffering is exceptional?
Maybe. Maybe not.
The times are strange, no doubt.
In the heat of it, what I believed
was the heat of it, I shouted like a dockworker
that I was unafraid. Come at me,

I hollered, you can only kill me
once. There is nothing left
to take. I've said that before. I still hear
the echo from when the flames
licked my feet,
my fearlessness a cabaret.

Of course, there is more to take.
I'm copious and so are you.
My pipe. My roses. My stubborn
mule. My burbling
brook which must be traversed
to get to the island of blue lawn chairs.

My loaded apple trees,
raspberry bushes, and prefab on a slab,
and memories of Petra, with three
teeth, who made a salsa just for me
when she saw me coming toward her
diner, Petra's. My high school drama

teacher, Jim, his hair bronze, his pallor
ruddy, his gait exceptional. I believe
we should marry, he said to me one night,
blowing smoke rings, driving me home
from play practice. I was Mary Warren
in *The Crucible*. I'd just learned

to insert a tampon. There were no
boundaries then, and Jim was queer.
His real love was the boy who played
The Boy in *The Fantasticks*.
I could feel my blood let down
like breast milk into the fabric

of his car seat. I loved the theater.
What luxury, putting on plays
in the middle of a cornfield.
The witch I played giving me
license to go into fits
in front of the student body.

Jim was fired, and died.
Petra's dead.
The berry bushes are a dream.
The island is a pipe dream.
The pipe is a hallucination.
Still, I'm copious, and so are you.

SIMILE

You can't be simile.
Deep down even
mud is not
comparable. I had a friend
whose smile was a frown.
My last paramour, my very
last, wore an atypical
cowboy hat. A bit of a rodeo
clown. Paranoid
about the whole area of the belly
button. People
are so unlike.
I had a side-eyeing dog.
A king forced
into a peasant's clothes. At the end,
and there is always an end in tales
of peasants, I'd look up and find him
staring bullet holes into my skull.
Not memorizing me.
Asking to be rescued from his plight.
Pain is the ultimate plight,
he might have said in a tale,
but he could not talk
until he came to my friend in a dream.
Promise you'll tell mother I miss her,
he said. And my friend fulfilled
her promise. I almost wrote
my friend fulfilled her primrose, an unlike
flower. Big-ovaried and hairy-stemmed,
old, fertile, femme.
My friend, who does not believe in portents,
still obeyed the talking dog.
This is her version of love, and it's her version
all the way down.
Death also incomparable, specific

only unto itself. Death to the dying must feel
so contrary to death's history, as the ego
dies hard. Mine. The hands curl in on themselves,
fern fronds. When I nursed my baby decades
back, moonlight poured in the window,
and starlight,
and I felt myself click into the template,
like a bone back into its joint,
doing what mothers do and have done.
Maybe I was painted on an urn somewhere.
Until later when the handle busted off
and the urn turned to dust and we were solidly,
brutally nothing
but ourselves.
When I taught figuration,
I said the simile, with its *like* and *as*, confesses
failure in its very nature. It can't transmogrify
a spoon into a fish or revivify
the marriage. We liked each other.
We like each other no more,
our loathing radical and strange.
Nor can it warm
the corpse and bring a throb back
to its temple. The shroud,
laundered and bleached,
returns to its essential nature, bedsheet,
with a mended scar
and a menstrual stain shaped unlike
any constellation of stars
and, goddamnit, I sleep on it.

PENETRALIUM

I wish I could tell you how deep
the suck goes,
how dark it is and holy,
its tragedies siloed. They dot
the landscape, with oxen, mud-hooved,

and crows.
Shakespearean but boiled-down,
a thick gravy, oversalted,
served on white bread, day-old,
sold cheap at the bakery outlet.

It broods on the woodland edge,
morbidly forested and bottle green,
fermented in swamp, dung, skunk,
and bridled by sorcery, potions,
Bible school puppetry, ogres, fairies,

poorly rendered papier-mâché
good and bad Samaritans.
Kept awake by raw, honest terrors,
eviction dreams, half-conscious
fantasies of terrible mothers wielding

hatchets, but oddly
free, like a free lunch is free,
or a vacant lot, or a stinkweed
bouquet. Just sit with it as you'd sit
with a legless drunk

who won't shut up about the bygone.
Don't bring your sobriety narratives
to this bedside, Diane.
Be drunk . . . it's the only way, raved
Baudelaire, corkscrewed

through and through with syphilis.
How artless, this source
of art, this shit show where
the greenest
watercress grows.

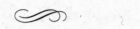

POETRY

There's no sense
in telling you my particular
troubles. You have yours too.
Is there value
in comparing notes?
Unlike Williams writing
poems on prescription pads
between patients, I have
no prescriptions for you.
I'm more interested
in the particular
nature and tenor of the energy
of our trouble. Maybe
that's not enough for you.
Sometimes I stick in
some music. I'm capable
of hallucination
so there's nothing wrong
with my images.
I'm not looking for wisdom.
The wise don't often write
wisely, do they? The danger
is in teetering into platitudes.
Maybe Keats was preternaturally
wise, but what he gave us
was beauty, whatever that is,
and truth, synonymous, he wrote,
with beauty, and not the same
as wisdom. Maybe truth
is the raw material of wisdom
before it has been conformed
by ego, fear, and time,
like a shot
of whiskey without
embellishment, or truth lays bare

the broken bone and wisdom
scurries in, wanting
to cover and justify it. It's really
kind of a nasty
enterprise. Who wants anyone
else's hands on their pain?
And I'd rather be arrested
than advised, even on my taxes.
So, what
can poetry be now? Dangerous
to approach such a question,
and difficult to find the will to care.
But we must not languish, soldiers,
we must go so far as to invent
new mechanisms of caring.
Maybe truth, yes, delivered
with clarity. The tone is up
to you. Truth, unabridged,
has become in itself a strange
and beautiful thing.
Truth may involve a degree
of seeing through time.
Even developing a relationship
with a thing before writing,
whether a bird
or an idea about birds, it doesn't
matter. But please, not only
a picture of a bird. Err
on the side of humility, though
humility can be declarative.
It does not submit. It can even appear
audacious. It takes mettle
to propose truth
and pretend it is generalizable.
Truth should sting, in its way,
like a major bee, not a sweat bee.
It may target the reader like an arrow,

or be swallowable, a watermelon
seed we feared as children
would take up residency in our guts
and grow unabated and change us
forever into something viny
and prolific and terrible.
As for beauty, a problematic word,
one to be side-eyed lest it turn you
to stone or salt,
it is not something to work on
but a biproduct, at times,
of the process of our making.
Beauty comes or it doesn't, as do
its equally compelling counterparts,
inelegance and vileness.
This we learned from Baudelaire,
Flaubert, Rimbaud, Genet, male writers
of the lavishly grotesque.
You've seen those living rooms,
the red velvet walls and lampshades
fringed gold, cat hair thick
on the couches,
and you have been weirdly
compelled, even cushioned,
by them. Either way,
please don't tell me flowers
are beautiful and blood clots
are ugly. These things I know,
or I know this is how
flowers and blood clots
are assessed by those content
with stale orthodoxies.
Maybe there is such a thing
as the beauty of drawing near.
Near, nearer, all the way
to the bedside of the dying
world. To sit in witness,

without platitudes, no matter
the distortions of the death throes,
no matter the awful music
of the rattle. Close, closer,
to that sheeted edge.
From this vantage point,
poetry can still be beautiful.
It can even be valuable, though
never wise.

BOBBY

All the actors from the sitcoms
I watched as a child are dead.
And the musicians assassinated
overdosed or natural
causes. Take a hint
they shout from the top tier
of the ancient Roman
amphitheater. No
I will not take a hint. I still
make a mean
bowl of soup which can now
be poured directly
from a can and inserted
into a box that heats
via electromagnetic radiation.
I once owned
a guitar and learned me
some of the chords to "Me
and Bobby McGee" and damn
if I couldn't sing
good.
My voice was not like Janis.
Nothing like Janis. It was high
serene
forthcoming
piercing
mezzo
very lyric
very trill
hugely skinny like a waterspout
the neighbors complained about
its beauty I sang I sung I'm singing
I barely began to begun
and I'm not done.

RHAPSODY

I like to call marriage state-sponsored
fucking. To return
to the world, I must learn
how to love the world again. My problem
is with the word *again*. I don't like repeat
performances. I come from a long line
of hungry people who hate leftovers.
The only movie I can watch more than once
is the original *Frankenstein*. I like the present
tense of spectacle. It's like eating

an oversour pickle. Wakes you up but hurts
your gonads. I got good
at romance early by choosing to wear pink
knee socks to the funeral. I sat on the floor
of the hearse on the ride from the church
to the cemetery, "making the best of it." That's
romance. It's like when my mother took me to see
Mary Poppins for my eighth birthday and it turned her
into a flaming bitch. I understand why you didn't like it,
I said to her, but I really loved it because I'm a kid.

Actually, I hated it as much as she did.
That's romance. Or when she went to the slaughterhouse
to pick up a cow heart for my science project.
It was still warm, wrapped in white paper.
They handed it over like a newborn and she gagged
all the way home. That's romance. Some poet wrote
that he adores economy and requires precision.
I actually looked for antonyms:
extravagance, ignorance, imprudence, negligence, squandering.
I felt like a poor kid who finds a quarter and gorges

themselves on penny candy. From then on, everything
I created or promoted would be rococo. Bows
and beams of sunlight festooning the candelabra
of the bewigged swing set. I have oppositional
poetry disorder. I want to express
my opinion about people expressing their opinions.
If only I could jump on the back of a motorcycle
and ride into the sweet-potato field, where the mother
deer flash their hooves and roar, and lay flat on the snake-laced
ground at midnight and watch the empty spectacle of the numb

satellites' mindless circling that looks a lot like a boob
who thinks they've found nirvana. And to observe
with a jaundiced eye the skunk family march in a line
out of the cedar swamp and eat crayfish from a washtub. I want a papa
bear to split the Tree of Life down the middle, scattering
the wormy apples. His furry berry-stained maw
such a display of what used to be called *reality*.
I want the next turn I make to be unearned.
Like getting gangbanged in a greenhouse at age fourteen
and calling it a honeymoon. I guess now that would be called

trauma, a word I've grown to hate. It's like a cute puppy
who got old and whose only new trick is shitting in the house,
or a Band-Aid they call "flesh-colored"
that only matches the flesh of the owner of the Band-Aid
company. A word can be overused into emptiness,
which is also a banality, so don't tell anyone you love them.
If you call fucking *making love*, I'll kill you in your sleep.
Don't say, *I do*. It's what suckers say, what liars say,
never take an oath wearing clothes that have to be hung
on padded hangers.

When women are murdered,
people on TV always comment on the victim's cheerfulness.
Like being a songful canary should have kept her
from getting her throat slit. My advice is to live on a street

in which no one will say, when you're murdered,
things like that don't happen here. Live in a neighborhood
where every house is considered a scar on the face
of France. My adult son calls me at noon to ask
if I ever loved his father. How can I
express that marital love is twelve banalities ago?

It's like asking if I liked the taste of peaches
when I was a toddler. I preferred
smoke, catalpa worms, bowling trophies,
and using tweezers to remove the lit-up ass of a firefly
so I could smear it around my finger like a wedding ring.
The adage is that a cynic is a broken romantic,
except for Arthur Rimbaud, who was born and died
a misanthropic shrew. I would like to conjecture
that a romantic is a cynic who has been infected
with resurrection metaphors and believes in the integrity

of a good
line break. I know
someone who saw a famous
lounge singer carried out
of a Vegas hotel
on a stretcher with a broken
light bulb in his ass.
Be that guy.
Don't be Jesus, be the Shroud.
Don't be the savior, be the stain.

LITTLE FUGUE WITH JEAN SEBERG AND TUPPERWARE

I've tired of them.
Those dishes I learned to cook for love.
Dishes that were not in my nature
but I suppressed my nature.
For love, for love.
What ridiculous things I've done.
I've said big dick when I meant small dick.
And you know? I've tired
of the French New Wave.
Did I ever love Jean-Paul Belmondo?
Now he seems like some trifling prick
I'd have to call into my office
for disrespecting teacher. I'm teacher.
I had no God-given authority.
I had to self-generate it, like God.
At some point, God had to take the leap
to become God.
Those dishes. I carried them in Tupperware
knockoff storage containers. Drove them
miles, through blizzards, for love.
Love, that little wood tick. That tick-in-the-ass.
Say the word enough times inside your head,
it will fall out of its meaning
like a stillborn, plop, into the toilet.
Even Jean Seberg, so intent on her prettiness.
Rocking the short hair.
Trifling waist. Trifling striped dress.
She died of miscarriage-trauma.
Miscarriage-trauma caused by the FBI.
It is better to get over things.
To forget the stupid recipe for fetus-in-a-jar.
So much of cinema, so much of it,
seemed like something I was supposed to like.
I oohed and aahed in all the right places.
A pretense of breathlessness.

But I sat there squirming. Embarrassed by the jump
cuts. The film where the heroine
cuts off her lover's dick and carries it
around with her in a knockoff
Tupperware storage container. God,
I tried to write papers about these things,
but I found no meaning in the meaning.
I'd focus on the little spaces between
the actor's teeth, or that the actress looked like
the empty-faced Jesus-seeking girls back home.
In the end, as he's dying, he tells her
she makes him want to puke.
Yes, sister, many-a-night has ended thusly.

THE PERSONAL

I who have loved the personal
have fallen a bit out of love
with the personal.

I have never
owned a pair of slippers.
I recently realized my feet are cold.
I think I'll buy slippers, I said
to myself and then to my son,

over the phone, just for the sake
of conversation. I wasn't asking
for his permission or anything.
Why do you want slippers? he asked.
I'm cold, I said. You're cold?

What's wrong with you? he asked,
like an accusation.
I don't like it that you're suddenly cold.
You sound like Ha-hoo, he said.
Ha-hoo was my grandmother.

I sent him a photo of some slippers
that didn't seem too bad. They look
like Ha-hoo, he said. You're
folding. You're caving, he said.
Get this—he's had slippers

for years. But I'm supposed to be
some sort of paragon. The slippers
I am maybe going to buy are the kind
that you can just slide your foot into.
Don't get those, my son said.

You'll fall down the stairs.
Thanks for the vote of confidence,
I said. He sent me a photo of some fake
moccasins lined in rabbit fur.
Get these, he said.

You've got to be kidding me,
I said. He knew I'd reject them
for being appropriative. And think
of the poor rabbit. He was playing
mind games. He learned that from

his years living on the streets.
I picture myself in a broken heap
at the bottom of the stairs.
Then I picture Ha-hoo skinning a rabbit.
Women back then had to have cold

hearts. Joyce James told me
the reason my milk wasn't coming in
after I gave birth was because
I'd washed greens for what seemed
like hours with my hands in ice cold water.

Everybody knows cold water dries up
your supply, she said, like I was a factory
or something. I miss the days when I had
a grandmother and no one personalized
anything I did. I'd sit in her closet

and put pebbles in her high heels
and she never said a word. My feet
were like hot coals back then.
I could go outside in the winter
without shoes and with every step

the snow would hiss and melt.
If I had an insight, I'd keep it bottled up
until it disappeared, and I didn't
have that many insights. Imagine
it. One pair of red shoes and no

slippers. My mind was empty
as a ballroom and I was not
compelled to dance.

UNTITLED

I can't title anymore.
It's like naming a baby "baby."
Or sticking a toe tag on a dead body
and labeling it "dead body," or "Random Jesus."
There are a multitude
of Random Jesuses beyond That Jesus.
There was a Jesus who won
a party boat on *The Price Is Right*.
He was a small man with stringy muscles,
but he picked up the male model
and hoisted him into the party boat.
Some natural order had been upended
and everyone, even the host, knew it.
There was a guy on the same show
with "Genghis" on his name tag.
He roared when he won a car
he could never have fit inside.
His vast body was lit up with joy.
There was something one-dimensional
about him. One-dimensional and wide,
like a symbol or a god.
If you name a woman "Teeny,"
will the body obey the name or rebel against it?
I knew a woman named Teeny who stole
silverware by hiding it in her pantyhose.
She was teeny but heavy as lead.

THE OTHER

I've fought it so hard, this
responsiveness to the other,
though as a child it was my nature
to teeter
on the edge of deathbeds and read
storybooks to the ones lying there.
Children, I think, are without ulterior motives.
Those come later, in conjunction with desire.
Maturity taught me to fight it,
that at-oneness with the sufferer. I felt good

about snatching myself back.
I had a life to live, things to lose, like my so-called
virginity, though I'd already lost it
to myself. I helped
a family friend, Jan, by then bald-headed Jan,
onto the bedside commode, and wiped her,
and got her back in bed.
Then I stopped visiting.
Her house had always been a respite.
When she got sick it became the scene of the crime.

I can still smell the sweet rot of her pee.
Like Peter
Pan I was youth! I was joy! I still had
my milk teeth.
I thought poems required a degree
of heartlessness, a running
away into the pines, to the streambed.
From that point on I became squeamish.
I could no longer dig
the bullets out of animals and brown

their thighs in butter and eat them,
or soak morels in a sink full of hot salt water
to kill the bugs hiding in their spongy hollows.
Once I declined a man's fig,
having heard gossip of the dead wasp
living at its center. And I have the audacity, now,
to ask people who serve the suffering
to serve with joy. Joy. What a joyless word.
As if I served the drug addicts in my life with joy.
As if I kissed the slashed wrists. The bored doctors.

I've only kissed one medical doctor in my life
and it was because he was young and I wanted
to pretend I was young again and he wanted
a green card. Now, when I think of doctors, I say,
out loud, don't touch me. I think of Pap smears.
They want to know what's inside me.
I once invented a dance, with a friend
who later died of AIDS in his early twenties.
The dance was called the Dance of the Bobby Pin,
and required the dancer to pass a bobby pin

from their lips into the lips of the other dancer
while mutually undulating like snakes.
No body parts touched. Not even the lips.
The bobby pin was the lone interface,
like the coupler linking two cars of a train.
It was fun. We got laughs from onlookers.
Once, he was drunk and stoned enough
to ask if he could feel my boobs.
He wasn't attracted to women.
His interest was purely clinical. Sure, I said,

go ahead. Feel them.
He found it to be an interesting experiment
in discovering neutrality.
He went blind before he died,

and recited the Lord's Prayer
in order to appease his mother.
At least I assume it was an appeasement.
Maybe deep, deep down beneath
the hipness and provocations, he was a true believer.
When he died, we hadn't talked in a while.

By then I'd married his archnemesis.
At the core of their hostilities was art.
Always art. The person I married was envious
of playfulness in art. Playfulness got all
of the attention, he claimed,
though he was the better draftsman.
He was likewise jealous of the Dance of the Bobby Pin.
It was all projection.
Especially the marriage and the divorce.
I cried in front of the judge,

but now I realize the tears were false,
like the tap water that poured
from the eyes of Tiny Tears, the weeping doll.
What I really wanted was to bury
a pickaxe in my husband's forehead.
With joy! With joy! With a surplus of joy!
Whatever grace you stumble upon,
don't sit on it like a smug hen on its eggs.
Whatever you think of yourself,
think otherwise, Diane.

BALLAD THAT ENDS WITH BITCH

She was one of those long-nosed ones.
Mary, full of grace, cream atop the milk.
I picked my way through dung piles and bones.
Animal dung. Animals of every ilk.

All of us come with a ballad.
Hers was set in an Amish puppy mill.
Born in a mill, then forced to give birth.
Birth before she'd been a year on this cold earth.

She rolled on her back to show me her scar.
Playing dead, she showed me her spaying scar.
I have one of those, I said, but mine is perpendicular.
Little princess, I too have been opened with a crowbar.

My tenderness. I couldn't find a way to say yes.
I felt splayed, my little scar exposed.
It's all against our will, I suppose.
I stumbled through brambles to find my way, I guess.

A whole pathless hillside covered in sedge.
Barn cats arched their backs, neutralizing agents.
Agents of indifference. Other animals pawed at the gate.
Looking to get in or out of grace or fate.

I walked her, using a piece of rope for a leash.
She knew nothing of a leash, that false umbilical cord.
On that tether, she wandered aimless, trampish.
Too small for this world, vast as a billboard.

I was once too small for this world.
Somebody burned my arm with a cigar.
They said they didn't know I was there.
I believe them. I still have the scar.

She was a prototype of tenderness.
I wandered that hillside, this way and that.
I could not find my way to yes.
She was a child bride in a plastic crèche.

As I drove away, her borders dissolved.
She dispersed herself across the landscape like mist.
Through the fog I could still see her belly scar.
A horizon line, I told myself, divvying up that and this.

When I returned to my digs, the house was frozen stiff.
A fine skim of hoarfrost on the writing desk.
Why call it a writing desk?
It's commerce-covered. Bills. Tat. That. This.

At age ten, I turned away from tenderness.
I remember the moment. A flipping of a switch.
My house is a cold mess except for that thing in the corner.
Poetry, that snarling, flaming bitch.

AGAINST POETRY

A poem, unlike
a living being, cannot
perceive you, and in
perceiving you, grant you
reality. If it sleeps
with you, it cuts you.
It runs a few
degrees cooler than room
temperature. A love poem
does not love you. Or
does not necessarily love
you. A love poem faces
outward. It performs
love adequately. Lately,
I've wondered about poetry's
efficacy. It's like doubting
a long romance, or romance
itself, the essence of it.
Fearsome, to doubt
your life's foundation.
I've also wondered about
painting. What distinguishes
a good or great painting,
paintings I've loved, from
illustration? Lately everything
seems illustrative to me,
as if the whole world
is a cunning metaphor.
A young painter once
cautioned me not to bring
a literary framework to visual art.
A sane admonition, I think.
Maybe what distinguishes
art from illustration
is its uselessness. Art,

useless at its core,
but not valueless. And
what is the correlation
between painting and poetry?
What makes a poem merely
illustrative, and what elevates it
to an essential artfulness,
i.e., uselessness? I know
I am using the old language
here. *Merely. Elevates.*
I am in an antiquated room.
Its fixtures, dust-covered
and ornate. Furniture,
having been built at the behest
of another era, from a principle
of design that forefronts beauty,
is delicate, as if balanced on a foal's
trembling legs. Maybe to live within
a poem is to entrap oneself
in an architecture constructed upon
outmoded theories of composition.
It's possible there is an undiscovered
room or house, or a structure
somewhere I don't yet have
the language for. An academy of silences.
A cathedral of cross-purposed
voices. A posthuman spaciousness
filled only with a reemerged
species of butterflies. A catacomb
of cluster flies. Whatever it will be,
it will be new, filled
with its own mystifying absurdities,
and likely beyond me.
This body may not be built
for it. Mine is the kind
of body you drag around
town on a leash, with a choke

chain. You don't love it,
but it's yours to contend with,
though it compresses your
soul. When did it begin
to compress rather than
liberate my soul? Early,
but I do remember
when it was my soul's instrument,
or indistinguishable from
my soul. I could sit on the front
stoop and the whole world
came streaming in through
the structures of my senses.
Maybe the body is the soul's
metaphor. Maybe to escape it
is to escape the service
economy. To dissolve analogy.
Attain uselessness.

LEGACY

I think of the old pipes,
how everything white
in my house is rust-stained,
and the gray-snouted
raccoon who insists on using
my attic as his pee pad,
and certain
sadnesses losing their edges,
their sheen, their fur
chalk-colored, look
at that mound of laundry,
that pile of pelts peeled away
from the animal, and poems,
skinned free of poets,
like the favorite shoes of that dead
girl now wandering the streets
with someone else's feet in them.

ROMANTIC POETRY

Now that the TV is gone and the music
has been hauled away,
it's just me here, and the muffling silence
a spider wraps around a living morsel.
And at times, often, the unbearable.
I bear it, though, just like you.
Long ago, I bore a suitcase filled with books,
bore it far on city streets. To sell, I guess, at some
used books place, one of those doorways down
steps into dankness and darkness. The scent

of mildewed, dog-eared, fingered pages.
The suitcase, big and square and sharp-cornered,
covered in snakeskin, bought at Goodwill
for a dollar, knowing I had some traveling to do,
some lugging, and I was right.
What books I sold I do not know.
Maybe that's where *Modern Poetry* went.
The cover cherry-red and blossom-white.
I can see its spine in my mind's eye,
pointing downward beneath the dank

and the dark to the water tunneling
under the city and making its way to the river.
Poems sliding down the book's spine
into water, the shock of the cold and dank,
down where my uterine lining, my blood
and cast-off ovulations, cast-off fetal
tissue swims, below the city.
The microdead ride modern poems
like swan boats in the park.
From the park to the river to the sea.

I'm thinking now of PJ Harvey and Nick Cave.
Balladeers. Lovers. Vita and Virginia.

Frank O'Hara and Vincent Warren. Somehow,
we ride our lost loves out to sea. Or they ride us.
It doesn't matter. Poet or poem or reader, the same
ectoplasm. The modern, in time, becomes antique,
and the stone faces of the dead convert to symbols,
ripe for smashing. Come to think of it,
symbols are terrible. As the tyrant
shouted to the masses,

part of his brainwashing campaign:
I know it, and you know it too.
I was twenty-three when I sold off
Modern Poetry and sailed to Italy, seeking
Romantic poetry, which was at one time
modern, and found my way to Rome,
and Keats's death room.
His deathbed, a facsimile.
Everything he touched was burned,
to kill what killed him.

I lifted his death mask from its nail,
cradled it, closed my eyes and kissed his lips
until the plaster warmed,
and stained his face
with the lipstick on my lips. Red
as the cover of *Modern Poetry.*
The color of the droplets of arterial blood
he coughed onto his sheets and viewed
by candlelight. Then he knew he was done for.
His death warrant, he called it.

After those many kisses over his face and eyes,
and the reticulated eyelashes,
cold and tangled,
my lips were blossom-white,
my face, chalked. Like I'd caught
something from him,

and I don't just mean consumption,
though my lungs burned for years.
They still burn.
This is the danger of the ecstasy of kissing

the dead or dying poet on the mouth.
The disease you'll catch—well,
it changes you.
The tingle in the spine,
the erotic charge, will be forever married
to poetry's previous incarnations.
It's why marriage itself never worked for me.
I kept wanting to get to the part
where death parts us
and I could find myself again.

Keats made such a compact corpse.
Only five feet tall, shorter than Prince,
and intricately made. Always,
he was working it, working it out,
the meaning of suffering, the world's,
his own, the encounter with beauty,
nearly synonymous with suffering,
how empathy could extinguish him,
and he could set down the suitcase at last,
or finally deliver him to himself, distinct

as the waves in his hair and the bridge
of his nose. How auspicious,
rare, lush,
bizarre, kinky, transcendent,
romantic, to be young, just twenty-three,
and to cradle him
in my arms, as we listened
to the burbling water
of the Fontana della Barcaccia
from the open window.

HIGH ROMANCE

And then Keats's ghost found
that he could no longer love
Fanny Brawne. He'd escaped
the body like a love
letter from its envelope, and he'd flown
like a love letter in a windstorm.
He'd seen that the words
formed from ink melted in the rain.
Words, he now knew—and he'd once been
such a devotee—didn't matter,
or didn't matter so much as he'd believed
they mattered. Something mattered, he knew,
but whatever it was he couldn't put
words to it, or he didn't have the heart
to put words to it. He did feel love,
but it was an arrow without a target.
It was diffuse, like an atomized
perfume, or stars as the poor see them,
who cannot afford glasses. He saw
that Fanny, as she was known,
was a concept, just as he had been a concept.
They each inhabited the same amount
of space, like a tablespoon
of butter and a tablespoon of lard.
In a book, they would each occupy
a single page. Their brains, encased
in cranial bones and flesh and heads of hair,
could each rest on a single, silk pillow.
Ideas, he found, don't die. Even notions fly
like cottonwood seeds through the air.
And love had been a notion. He saw
that Fanny, in time, would slip free of herself,
everything does, in time, even roses,
even stones, foothills, fleas, and poems.
Rhyme, he saw, existed on its own behalf.

He could catch it like a bird catches
an air current. From above, he could see
that Fanny was not trifling. Nothing,
from above, is trifling, nor more compelling
than anything else. His love for her, he saw,
had been an invention of the mind.
Only belief could sustain it, but he
could no longer sustain belief. Now
and then he'd try it on again—love—
like a fancy hat he could not afford
and now appeared ludicrously overdesigned.
Once, his ghost managed to look at her again,
through the gauzy curtains that hung
over her bedroom window. His gaze
was too objective to find her beautiful,
but objectivity itself—that was beautiful.

LOVE LETTER

But what can it be if love is a past-
tense event? And what
was love then
according to my brain
and what
is love now and how do I direct it
like a beam with the power
to excise all that is not love? For a time
I believed getting and keeping
love required lace. Procuring lace
and arranging it
on my body in a certain way.
Isn't that funny and/or strange?
I modulated my voice to the northern
region of its register. Reddened
my lips. This was love's drapery
and music and face.
If you've read *Madame Bovary*, if you've read
gothic romance, you know
the denouement of that arc.
When I first read the word *denouement*
out loud, my ex-husband
laughed at my mispronunciation.
I include it here as an illustration
of the fact that love does not conquer
all. Now when I think
of love, it's like focusing too hard
on the mechanisms of blinking or breathing.
You can be blinded or suffocated
by that degree of self-consciousness.
Like a love letter, love seems to me to exist
on a thin plane, a disintegrating page
covered in words scratched
onto the surface with purple disappearing ink
cooked up in a chemistry lab.

I'm sure I've written a love letter here
and there. Something gauche,
a performance designed toward
the specific outcome of eternity.
I read of a feral dog who could only be captured
by putting the soiled blankets of her puppies
in a live trap. This is my metaphor for a love letter.
I own a letter my father wrote my mother
when they were newly in love.
The stationery is smallish and decorated
with a garish deep red rose in aching
bloom. He spends most
of his language's currency bemoaning
his bad spelling. No wonder
she found him charming. For my people
it is the flaw that counts, but not for all
people. Our narrative is an object
lesson in the fact that flawed people
deserve to be loved, at least for a while.
That's the ephemeral part.
I'm much too sturdy now to invest
in the ephemeral. No, I do not own lace
curtains. It's clear we die a hundred times
before we die. The selves
that were gauzy, soft, sweet, capable
of throwing themselves away
on love, died young. They sacrificed
themselves to the long haul.
Picture girls in white nighties jumping
off a cliff into the sea. I want to say,
don't mistake this for cynicism,
but of course, it is cynicism.
Cynicism is a go-to I no longer have
the energy to resist. It's like living
with a vampire. Finally, just get it
over with, bite me. I find it almost
offensive to use the word *love*

in relation to people I actually love.
The word has jumped off
so many cliffs into so many seas.
What can it now signify?
Shall I use the word *affinity*
like J. D. Salinger, not a good
man, put into the mouths
of his child-genius characters? I have
an affinity for my parents. An affinity
for you. I will make sure you are fed
and clothed. I will listen to you
endlessly. I will protect your privacy
even if it means removing myself
from the equation. Do those sound like
wedding vows? Are they indiscriminate?
Well, then, I am indiscriminate.
I am married to the world.
I have worked it all out in front of you.
Isn't that a kind of nakedness?
You have called for a love letter.
This is a love letter.

GERTRUDE STEIN

I'd just brushed the dog, there on the dog's couch.
I was wearing a black—well, to call it a gown is a criminal
overstatement—a black rag. It became clear to me—

and when I say clear I mean the moment went crystal cathedral—
I could see my life from—not a long shot—
but what they used to call an increment apart—a baby step

to the right or left of myself—about the width of a corrective
baby shoe. There I was, broad-shouldered, witch-shaped
without the associated magic—with my dog in my shack—

once mauve faded to pink—beyond sex or reason—
a numbness had set in—Gertrude Stein, Picasso's portrait of her—
that above-it-all—or within-it-all—look on—not a face

but the planes that suggest a face—the eyes
aren't really lined up right or the real eyes are peering
from behind the cutout shapes of eyes. The couch

had been a sort of—not a gift—but a donation of sorts
from a person with plenty of money. When it was dragged
into my house it was already—stately—but with worn patches

and stains. A trinity of dogs over time had laid claim to it—
three egotists. To brush the dog meant I had to visit it
in its monarchy—and in that visit—that single prismatic

increment—I saw I'd become—maybe all arrive in their own time—
some before dying, some after—a draped artifact—
haystack or headstone rising out of the plains—

and then, with fascination—and a degree
of sadness and even objectivity—I loved—
as I once loved *Tender Buttons*—myself.

ROMANTIC POET

You would not have loved him,
my friend the scholar
decried. He brushed his teeth,
if at all, with salt. He lied,
and rarely washed
his hair. Wiped his ass
with leaves or with his hand.
The top of his head would have barely
reached your tits. His pits
reeked, as did his deathbed.

But the nightingale, I said.

ACKNOWLEDGMENTS

The Academy of American Poets *Poem-a-Day*— "Ballad," "Folk Song"

The Adirondack Review—"Modern Poetry," "Colette," "Threnody,"
   "Coda," "Pop Song" (as "Meet-Up")

The Adroit Journal—"An Aria"

AGNI—"Ballad That Ends with Bitch"

The Best American Poetry—"Little Fugue State," "Modern Poetry"

Chicago Review—"Poetry," "Another Ballad"

Couplet Poetry—"Ballad in Sestets"

In the Tempered Dark: Contemporary Poets Transcending Elegy—
   "Ballad That Ends with Bitch," "Pop Song," "Threnody"

Iterant—"Little Fugue State," "Bluish," "Untitled," "Little Refrain"
   (as "Small Refrain")

The Massachusetts Review—"My Education," "Simile," "Villanelle"

The New Republic—"Ballad from the Soundhole of an Unstrung Guitar,"
   "Comma," "Penetralium"

The New York Review of Books—"Curl," "Weeds"

The New Yorker—"Gertrude Stein," "High Romance," "Romantic Poetry"

Ninth Letter—"Rhapsody"

The Paris Review—"Legacy"

Peste Magazine—"The Other"

Poetry—"Allegory," "Bobby," "Romantic Poet," "Cowpunk," "Juke"

Pushcart Prize XLII: Best of the Small Presses—"Ballad That Ends
   with Bitch"

River Mouth Review—"Love Letter"

Under a Warm Green Linden—"Little Fugue with Jean Seberg and
   Tupperware"

The Yale Review—"Monody," "Against Poetry"

With gratitude to all the tremendous professionals at Graywolf Press, es-
pecially to my Reader, Jeff Shotts.

Deep appreciation to my teachers, both inside and outside of the class-
room, especially Stephanie Gauper, who taught me there is such a thing as

a woman writer, and Conrad Hilberry, who tried to school me in Modern Poetry, and became a lifelong mentor and loving poet-comrade.

Thank you to my dear friends for your support, connection, conversation, and understanding. And always, to my people on the other side of the grass, who stick around.

Love and respect to my family for their constant support: Norma, my mom, Deb, my sister, Dewey, my brother-in-law, and Dylan, my son. And to my father, omnipresent in memory.

To the poets of the past, the known and the unknown, who struggled to keep poetry alive, especially the Young English Poet who loved violets, and now sleeps beneath them.

DIANE SEUSS is the author of six poetry collections, including: *frank: sonnets*, winner of the Pulitzer Prize, the National Book Critics Circle Award, the Los Angeles Times Book Prize, and the PEN/Voelcker Award; *Still Life with Two Dead Peacocks and a Girl*, a finalist for the National Book Critics Circle Award and the Los Angeles Times Book Prize; and *Four-Legged Girl*, a finalist for the Pulitzer Prize. She received a Guggenheim Fellowship in 2020 and the John Updike Award from the American Academy of Arts and Letters in 2021. Seuss was raised by a single mother in rural Michigan, which she continues to call home.

The text of *Modern Poetry* is set in Adobe Garamond Pro.
Book design by Rachel Holscher.
Composition by Bookmobile Design & Digital
Publisher Services, Minneapolis, Minnesota.
Manufactured by Friesens on acid-free,
100 percent postconsumer wastepaper.